MORE MARMADUKE

by
BRAD ANDERSON

published by
WYNDHAM PUBLICATIONS

A Target Book
Published in 1976
by Wyndham Publications Ltd.
A Howard & Wyndham Company
123 King Street, London W6 9JG

First published in the U.S.A. by
Scholastic Book Services,
a division of Scholastic Magazines, Inc.,
by arrangement with United Feature Syndicate, Inc.

Printed in Great Britain by
Richard Clay (The Chaucer Press) Ltd, Bungay, Suffolk

ISBN 0 426 11594 5

TO
The late Phil Leeming, who had a way of seeing dogs in funny
situations and wrote all those hilarious gags when Marmaduke
was the biggest pup in comics . . .
AND TO
Dorothy Leeming, his wife, who remains a part of The World
of Marmaduke.

*'Marmaduke' has been appearing in the London Evening News
since 1963, as well as other provincial newspapers*

"Keep your eyes open for a big dog.
He's a real trouble-maker."

"He's just found out 'Lassie's' been cancelled."

"Thanks to Marmaduke and a stray cat, the
principal gave us the rest of the day off."

"Cut the 'faithful dog at his master's feet' act . . .
What have you been up to?"

"If I strolled in two hours late for dinner I'd
never hear the end of it."

"Do you get out of that chair or do we have a confrontation?"

"Drop back behind this car again . . . I want another look!"

"If you don't mind, Marmaduke, I think everybody
would prefer my pot roast."

"The safest thing to do is to assume he got a large inheritance and can afford to buy it."

"I'll decide who is next if you don't mind!"

"Another parking ticket! You know you're
not supposed to be here!"

"So that's where he's been hiding his bones."

"One thing about taking Marmaduke along on a picnic . . . you appreciate the ants."

"Let him carry the books. You carry the lunch."

"I demand to know who's working on my car."

"When I told you to clean Marmaduke's house I didn't mean for you to go this far."

"Must you stop short like that?!"

"He weighs seventy pounds. At least part
of him does!"

"He decided to go through a car wash."

"Now do you believe there are mice in the kitchen?"

"I hate to think what is going to happen to the
poor cuckoo bird when he pops out this time."

"Must you turn up the thermostat every time you come in from the cold?"

"I left a plate of stuff I was mixing called
Marmaduke Surprise. Who ate it?"

"I don't think I'd tailgate, if I were you."

"He just *laughs* at any other punishment!"

"No, no, nurse! The tranquilizer is for me!"

"I don't want to hang up, Helen . . . but I
think I'd better!"

"Lois, what was the name and address of those
people at camp who had the big dog?"

"I don't usually give tickets to dogs but in his
case I'm going to make an exception!"

"Can you do something? He swallowed a transistor radio tuned to a rock station!"

"You wait right here. I have a sure cure for
your hiccups."

"I've caught him! What do we do now?"

"SIT!"

"He likes to wrestle. Keep him busy
until I make a sale."

"Here's a good one! I threw a bone on an inter-
state truck . . . Marmaduke's probably still
chasing it!"

"And don't think you can talk me
out of giving you a bath!"

"OK, OK, you've talked me out of it!"

"He doesn't seem to want to go out tonight!"

"You're new on this beat, so I'd better tell
you about your first *big* mistake."

"They're nice people . . . otherwise."

"I don't care if it is Marmaduke's idea! You're not putting a bone on top of the Christmas tree!"

"This time I'm going to draw the line!"

"Next time you're going to mind your own
business, let me know before I pick a fight!"

"Marmaduke! He's getting paid by the hour!"

"Next time, don't wear a hat that looks so delicious!"

"I will *not* trade bites!"

"Dottie! Turn the TV off! Marmaduke's carried away by the wrestling again."

"And now, the supreme test."

"Keep him away from my water bed!"

"From now on don't bring me my slippers!"

"Oh, no! Now I've seen everything . . .
Toasted bones!"

"There's the reason this is a low crime rate area."

"Is this the view you said was so fabulous?"

"I just hope you can put the meat away before
he does!"

"He fetched my slippers, but now he won't give them to me!"

"Cease fire! Hit him and we're all in trouble!"

"Please! One at a time!"

"Hey, it echoes in here! It echoes in here!"

"Hold it! I'm too tired to be welcomed home!"

"That's not fair, Marmaduke. You emptied it
before I could even get my straw in."

"It can't be spring fever . . . it must be winter
lethargy . . ."

"Next thing you know, he'll want dinner music."

"He's a great help in rounding up the boys for
choir practice."

"What I don't like is when he comes to a
screeching halt!"

"It sounded easy, didn't it — a spoonful every hour?"

"Suppose we decide we don't want to be forgiven?"

"Marmaduke treed a motorcycle."

"Wow! Am I glad you stopped! Marmaduke's
been chasing you for fifteen blocks!"

"How can you write a ticket without a ticket book?"

"Yeah, yeah, Marmaduke is chasing a kitty.
So . . . what else is new?"

"That isn't a very good way to try to communicate!"

"For the last time, *no!* You cannot join my team
of reindeer!"

"Marmaduke really isn't too smart . . . he can't even spell dog right."

"Thanks for carrying my briefcase,
Marmaduke . . . but next time give me time
to let loose of it!"

"Are you *sure* it's my turn to see if he's still there?"

"What does it LOOK like we're doing? We're
fighting over who gets the chair!"

"You can be replaced by a hamster, you know!"

"We spent his first year trying to make him understand us. Since then, we've been trying to understand *him*."

"Change a twenty?"

"Yes, sir . . . of course, sir!"

"Did you ask if you could invite your friends to
the birthday party?"

"GRRRRRR . . ."

"Uh . . . let's wait 'til we find a trash can . . ."

"You go right back and tell Mrs. Yates I don't
know what to do with you either."

"Don't laugh. He's had three scholarship offers
this week alone!"

"I told you not to make friends with that dog. Now how do you suppose we're going to get a 500-pound Great Dane off the roof?"

"OK, so you brought my slippers. Stop hamming it! They didn't taste that bad!"

"Has anybody seen the steaks I put out to thaw?"

"Miss his block on the opening day of the season,
and you're in real trouble!"

"That's the first car I ever saw that died from fright!"

"Does he get a proper diet?! He gets more
nourishment in an hour than I get in a week!"

"You don't often see a reunion like this."

"No, I'm not looking for tonsils . . . I think he ate my stethoscope."

"Don't stand under the mistletoe . . . he knows
what it means . . ."

"This is the part of the day I dread most . . .
getting home!"

"Nobody's going to snatch *that* purse!"